Summary and Analysis of "The Slight Edge: Turning Simple Disciplines into Massive Success and Happiness" by Jeff Olson

Summary Station

Table of Contents

Summary of The Slight Edge

The first edition of "The Slight Edge" by Jeff Olson was published in 2005. The most recent edition, the 8th edition published in 2013, has been extended with additional material and stories from readers of the previous editions of the book. It also allows an insight into how continuously applying the slight edge to his own life has made a difference in the lives of others.

"The Slight Edge" falls into the category of personal development/self-help books, and the gist of it is that you can achieve all your goals if you approach them with the right attitude.

In the following sections, you will find an outline of the main points Jeff Olson makes in each chapter, followed by some paragraphs about whether the book can really have the promised effect on the reader.

Chapter 1

In the first chapter, Jeff Olson introduces his readers to the idea that every single person on this planet has the potential to either turn into a poor, unsuccessful beach bum, or into a successful entrepreneur with a huge balance on his bank account. He tells his own story – about how he went from failure to success to another failure, and how he slowly learned that failure and success both happen for the same reason, and that this one single reason can either work for or against you, depending on how you use it. The reader is motivated by reading on because they would like to know more about the idea that people have complete control about the direction their life is taking.

Chapter 2

Many readers of "The Slight Edge" will have read other self help and personal development books. Many of those books promise to hold the secret to success and to a happy life. Mr. Olson describes how most people who buy such books find the ideas intriguing and apply them for a while. But then they stop and complain about all the techniques not working. He explains that all the wanting, wishing, and positive thinking in the world does not help people with achieving their goals unless they have "the first ingredient" to success.

Jeff Olson takes away the belief that failure is not an

option, and that positive thinking and wishing is all you need. He mentions a variety of examples of famous people who only came to their success after many failures (e.g. Edison and his light bulb). He explains that the missing ingredient to success is a person's own philosophy, i.e. the attitude behind their actions.

The right philosophy leads a person to the right attitude, the right actions, and the right results. This results in a good, successful life. While the wrong philosophy leads to the opposite.

The lesson from chapter 2 is nicely summarized in a quote within the chapter:

"Success is the progressive realization of a worthy ideal. Successful people do what unsuccessful people are not willing to do."

Chapter 3

The lesson of chapter 3 is introduced by a fable about twins who were offered the same choice by their dying father: they could either immediately get one million dollars, or one penny which will double every single day for one month. Another parable told is the story of the water hyacinth that wanted to reach the other side of a pond, and did so by doubling its mass every single day.

The moral of both stories is that little, humble beginnings can lead to bigger results. In regard to the two twins, the twin who took the million ended up being in debt, while the twin who chose the penny ended up with over ten million at the end of the month.

By using a variety of interesting stories, Jeff Olson shows the readers – and makes them understand – how small, simple habits and humble beginnings can over time lead to a fantastic quality of life. But he also shows how the opposite can happen to people for whom it's easier to not start with small habits, and who keep to the bad habits which over time lead to a reduced quality of life.

Chapter 4

What would you say if you learned that only about 1 in 20 people are successful with achieving their goals for life? It's roughly about 5% - and Jeff Olson would like the readers of his book to belong to this 5%. He explains that being among the 5% has nothing to do with your education, how much money you have in your account, how good you look, and how many people support you. To the readers, it should come as a relief to learn that they themselves are enough to work towards their dreams – without support, without money, without education. The message is:

You are enough as long as you are willing to start and stick to the simple tasks.

The challenge is in "mastering the mundane". Many people simply fail because they expect that they have to do something important, something earth-shattering to make their dreams come true. Jeff Olson states that this is not so. He explains that it is turning small, seemingly insignificant tasks into habits which will lead to bigger successes.

He also explains why people do not apply the slight edge (i.e. doing what unsuccessful people are unwilling to do):

- *Reason 1:* The things are easy to do – but also easy not to do.

- *Reason 2:* The results are invisible, often for a long time. People these days are used to instant gratification, so it is easy for them to give up after a brief period of time.

- *Reason 3:* Their habits seem insignificant. People

feel like those small, consistent actions can't make a difference.

Chapter 5

There is more good news for readers who doubted themselves after trying things like "The Secret" and similar self help books that make the readers believe they only have to will something into existence. For Jeff Olson, it's not the will who is one's ally – but time. He compares the achieving of goals with the traditional harvest: first you sow, then you let it grow (which can take quite some time), and then you harvest it.

The trick is not to wish for something really badly; the trick is to add little positive actions on the right side of the scale of your life. Even if the negative side on your scale is fuller at the moment, Jeff Olson explains, you can always change it with time as an ally. You simply have to add to the positive side with small positive actions, and stop adding to the negative side by eliminating the small negative habits. He stresses how important it is to "go slow to go fast". Constant, small actions add up, and over time you tip the scale to your favor.

Chapter 6

The following chapter continues the explanation about how people become disappointed because they expect a quantum leap, but do not get it in their own lives. He shows various examples of people who are seen as successful – but he also shows that they did not achieve their fame over night. The success of famous people might seem sudden, but once you have a closer look, you will notice that many small, constant steps have led to that final breakthrough.

Jeff Olson would like his readers to realize that once they stopped waiting and hoping for a miracle, they could become the miracle themselves and make their dreams come true.

Chapter 7

Chapter 7 explores the psychology of happiness, and shows how psychology in the past usually focused on what was wrong with people and how to treat problems like depression. The last decade has seen a shift towards positive psychology, i.e. observing what makes people happy and how people can achieve more happiness in their lives. The movement of happiness psychology was started in the year 2000 by a man called Seligman, and it gained more and more momentum every year.

One theory behind the happiness psychology is that happiness does not occur through having certain things but is created through many so-called happy habits. Success, they say, does not lead to happiness, but happiness does lead to success. In general, people need to be happy before they can achieve truly outstanding and lasting positive results in their lives.

Mr. Olson describes how positive psychology is the perfect partner for positive philosophy, aka the slight edge. It actually was a very important ingredient to make the slight edge work.

"Slight edge + happy habits," he says, "equal success."

To make it easier for readers to get started, Jeff Olson lists Shawn Achor's five happy habits, and asks the readers to choose at least one of those habits – and do it daily until it becomes a habit:

1. Write down 3 things you are grateful for every single day of your life. The catch: you can't simply write down the same 3 things every day.

2. Spend two minutes with writing about something happy that occurred within the last 24 hours.

3. Meditate daily, even if you only have a few minutes for it.

4. Practice one act of kindness every day – and don't expect anything in return.

5. Exercise for 15 minutes.

Chapter 8

Once the readers apply the slight edge into their lives, the author explains, they will create a ripple effect that also helps other people to make positive changes in their lives. He tells the readers that this might also come with some unexpected side-effects, one of them being responsibility: "Achieving greatness – in anything -isn't simply a matter of taking the steps that get you there. It is also a matter of paying the price. And the price is responsibility."

One single person who takes the right steps can have an immense impact on the world around him or her – but that person also has to accept that great success comes with great responsibility towards the community.

Chapter 9

In chapter 9, Jeff Olson stresses again how important it is to make a start even if it is a small beginning. Sometimes you might even discard something great as a piece of rubbish like Stephen King did with the beginning of his masterwork "Carrie".

The biggest successes have humble beginnings – the mere difference between a failure and a success is to start, even if it is only a very tiny step. Small steps take you somewhere, no steps take you nowhere.

Chapter 10

Examples on how little actions can change whether the curve of your life is going up or down can be as insignificant as pressing the snooze button in the morning. You can use those ten minutes to just be lazy, or you can get up and do something to move your life into the direction you would like it to take.

There is no standing still in life. You either move towards success or towards failure. In the beginning, the difference might be invisible, but you always move one way or the other.

Chapter 10 also explores how people are conditioned

towards being negative. He claims that we hear the word "yes" to our questions and wishes only 5,000 times, while we hear the word "no" over 40,000 times. Jeff Olson stresses that it is important that we learn to ignore the negativity because there will always be people who are going to say "no" to us, wanting to turn us down.

Unsuccessful people blame other people, their lack of chances, their lack of money, and their circumstances. Successful people keep their power (and don't give it away by blaming everyone and everything), and accept that as long as they say "yes" to themselves, they have the power to make the difference in their life.

Jeff Olson accepts that some people have past experiences that might be very negative, but he also says that it is not something to linger in. He tells his readers to learn from the past, but not to live in it. People should take lessons and experience from the past, but never see the past as an anchor that keeps them connected to all the negativity.

In chapter 10, Mr. Olson would like his readers to have an honest look at the different areas in their life, and think about whether this area of life is going up or down:

- Health (how fit are you, how often do you get sick etc.)

- Happiness (how happy are you in life?)

- Relationships (not just relationships with a love partner, but also friendships, work mates, your boss, family and other people who play a role in your life)

- Personal development (are you turning into a better person each day, do you stand still, or are you on the way down?)

- Finances (this is not just about the balance on your bank account, but also about the overall state of your financial affairs, i.e. mortgages, debts)

- Career (are you working in a job you love, do you

move towards the position you would like to have, do you earn enough money?)

- Positive impact on the world (do you influence people in a good or bad way? Are you a good role model? What will your legacy be?)

He explains that the reader always has the chance to make a positive change if he or she doesn't like the direction one of the areas is taking, and that a positive change will also have a positive impact on the other areas.

Chapter 11

By using the example of actual baby steps, Jeff Olson would like to show his readers how we were all capable of mastery even when we were babies. Baby steps show that mastery does not happen in one big leap – but that it can involve quite a few failed tries and falls until you are able to get up and walk with confidence. He would like people to understand that mastery is not something that waits for you at the end of the path, but that the path itself is the mastery, and that mastery lies right in the beginning: with the right state of mind, and the right attitude.

Mr. Olson shows how we forget about being masters of

our own destiny when we are adults. Figuratively speaking, we continue crawling instead of getting up and walking towards our goals.

He explains why this is so: it is because the world can be very harsh to people who speak about their dreams, and who even dare to take steps towards it. In extreme cases, people have been shot for speaking about a better world. Other people have been sentenced to death because of their desire to better the world (e.g. Socrates).

Your dreams are like magnets though. They continue pulling at you; they want you to walk towards them. For some people, however, it is easier to simply forget their dreams, to get rid of that pull and live a life that is acceptable by others.

Olson writes that "it means embracing living uncomfortably in order to attain a life that is genuinely comfortable – not deceptively comfortable".

He tells the reader about how he realized that what other people think does not matter in the end. He learned that an average person's funeral only makes about ten people cry. And some people don't even turn up for the funeral when the weather is bad. Mr. Olson himself then realized that it is only the people who truly followed their dreams that are truly missed. He asks the reader: If people don't care about you when you die, and can't even be bothered to come to your funeral when the weather is bad, then why should you not live the life you truly want to live and attract people who actually would care?

Chapter 12

Chapter 12 tells the reader that the best investment is into one's own personal development, and to fill one's brain with useful information. Accumulating knowledge is not enough; however, you also need to know how to apply it. Olson describes that the best method for personal development is a mix of knowledge that comes from learning, from experience, and from having a mentor. You don't only need to have the knowledge, but you also need to be able to put it into action – and the best way to learn this is to see one of the masters at work, i.e. seeing how things can be done successfully. By doing so, Olson writes, the reader also learns that getting from A to B is usually not a straight road, and that you often have to adjust your course.

You also need to be aware of your thoughts because you are the most influential person in your life. Your inner voice is always talking to you, and it can talk to you in a positive or negative manner. Use that influence on yourself wisely.

And this is the main reason why Jeff Olson places such a big importance on self improvement via personal development: by learning more, by widening your horizon, you will also change the way you think.

There are two types of thinking: conscious thinking, which is easily distracted and usually only focuses on one thing at a time, and unconscious thinking, which never loses track, has access to everything you know at all times and is the place where you create habits over time.

Your unconscious thinking is your auto-pilot, and Olson stresses how important it is that this auto-pilot is trained to keep us on the right track. This can only happen if you use your conscious thinking to create actions with intentions, and then repeat them again and again consciously, until your unconscious mind also accepts the new positive habits as something regular in your life.

Chapter 13

The five people who are closest to you have the most influence on the direction your life is taking. Chapter 13 focuses on how important it is to be surrounded by the right people, and how the laws of association can either have a positive or negative impact on your development.

Olson asks the readers to become aware of whose characteristics they take on, and who they are modeling. What direction are the people around you headed in, and is it a direction you would like to take, too?

The reader is encouraged to find people who also want to be part of the 5%, and to practice "compassionate awareness", i.e. the reader can be compassionate but also have his or her own direction in life.

Chapter 14

In chapter 14, Olson introduces the four slight edge forces
that are your allies if you just use them (otherwise they
work against you). They are momentum, completion,
refection and celebration.

- *Momentum*: Think of Newton's second law of
  thermodynamics. Olson describes how steady
  movement is better than growing too quickly and
  then crashing without ever getting up again.

- *Completion*: It is important to finish the incomplete
  things in your life, e.g. paying bills, replying to
  letters or emails. This is because incomplete things

always draw you back into the past. It is best to get them out of your life and completed as quickly as possible − because the past is not something you want to be drawn back to. Olson recommends spending 15 minutes a day actively completing things.

- *Reflection*: Being productive and being busy is not the same thing. This is why it is important that you take some time to reflect on what you have done every day. You might have been busy, but did you really achieve something? Olson explains that it is better for you to write down what you actually DID do at the end of the day, instead of making a to-do list in the morning. He also recommends that you should find a buddy or mentor if you can't do this on your own.

- *Celebration*: When you catch yourself doing

something right, even if it is something that seems

unimportant and inconsequential, acknowledge it.

Chapter 15

In this chapter, the reader learns about the power of habits, and what kind of positive habits he or she should adapt in their lives. Ovid said that nothing was stronger than a habit, and according to Olson, he was quite right about that. Unfortunately people tend to overlook good habits and ignore that bad habits have an accumulative effect over time as well. Add the problem that you can't change your habits unless you know about them.

The best way to get rid of your unwanted habits is to override them with positive habits. This is the point where Olson introduces the seven positive habits:

1. Show up

2. Be consistent, i.e. show up every day

3. Be committed for the long haul, i.e. don't just show up every day for a week. Ask yourself whether you are willing to spend thousands of hours to work towards your goals.

4. Have a positive outlook. No, this does not mean that you have to be happy all the time. It just means that you can't let negative emotions tear you down.

5. Stoke the fire of your desires with faith, i.e. you need to be able to see that you can achieve your goals. You need to have a vision and not just a vague dream.

6. Be willing to pay the price (i.e. give up something that consumes too much of your time but does not add any value)

7. Practice slight edge integrity, i.e. don't just act like a

successful person when people are watching. Stick to your values when nobody is watching because that's the time when it counts.

Chapter 16

In chapter 15, vague dreams were mentioned, and that you actually need to have a proper vision. In chapter 16, this is explained in more detail. Mr. Olson explains how a goal is nothing but a dream with a deadline added to it. He says that your goals need to be specific, that they need a deadline, and that you need to write them down, and add a plan to them. This should be done in three steps:

- *Step 1*: Write your dreams down (the description, and the deadline for it). Don't just fantasize about it. Make it concrete. "Dreams are goals with deadlines".

- **_Step 2_**: Look at it every single day. You need to constantly remind your brain and your unconscious thinking about where you are headed, so when your auto-pilot takes over, it takes you into the right direction. Only then "a series of events will kick in, including circumstances you could never have dreamed of".

- **_Step 3_**: Start with a plan. It doesn't have to be perfect. It does not have to be very elaborate, but it has to exist, it has to have a first step – and you have to take that first step.

Chapter 17

Assume nothing. People make the mistake of having assumptions about everything, and this hinders most people in making their dreams come true. Olson recommends that you try the slight edge, but also warns that the results don't just appear out of nowhere like promised in other self help books. He repeats that you need to write down your dreams in detail (don't just write you want a house but describe the house, the rooms, the location, the decorations), and then create a simple plan to move towards your dream. Then you need to find just one simple routine that you can add to your life on a daily basis.

Chapter 18

In the final chapter of the book, Olson provides the reader with a short summary of the three things he or she needs to do to successfully so that they can apply the slight edge in their lives:

- Have concrete goals

- Stick to positive, daily habits

- Surround yourself with the right people

He then ends with a short conclusion, encouraging the readers once more.

Final Pages

On the final pages, Jeff Olson greets the curious readers who skip to the end of the book by telling them that this book is a bit like life: You don't just skip to the end of it, but you have to work your way through it.

Then a long list of recommended books from the genres of personal development and self help follows. After all, Jeff Olson recommends that one of the readers' daily habits should be to read ten pages of a book that can have a positive influence in their lives.

Analysis of The Slight Edge

The "Slight Edge" presents some very valuable concepts to the reader, but the book in itself could be a lot shorter. The different concepts can be summarized in a few sentences:

- Successful people do the small things that people without success who often fail are not willing to do.

- Those small things can be as simple as getting up on time without pressing the snooze button, reading ten pages of a good book each day, doing fifteen minutes of exercise, or writing 500 words on your novel.

- People who take one little step at a time, and take one of those little steps every day even if the steps seem inconsequential, will reach their goals without fail. They simply have to keep doing the productive things without fail – no matter whether they feel like it or not.

- You need clearly defined goals with a deadline, because if you don't have clear goals you will never be able to reach them.

Jeff Olson wrote a book that is easy to read and all the stories and examples can provide helpful motivation to people who are not yet "there" (i.e. willing to take the little steps), however, the book sometimes appears to just stretch the few important points over many chapters. It takes the author a long time to get to the point in each chapter. Often the reader will get the idea before the author spells it out. This often achieves the effect that the reader thinks "Yes, I know what you want to say. So why don't you just say it and move on to the next point?"

Can the Slight Edge really make a difference in people's life?

"The Slight Edge" by Jeff Olson is a personal development book that makes sense, and is not filled with empty promises. In recent years, the readers have been bombarded with books that promise you the world if you only believed enough. This led to many disappointed people, to many broken hearts, to many people thinking that they simply did not want their dream strongly enough. Jeff Olson does it differently – and he does it so in a refreshingly honest way. He is upfront right from the beginning. He tells his readers that they are in full control of their lives, but that wishful thinking alone doesn't take them anywhere.

Through the honest observations of life, and through the author's own experiences, he created a book that is filled with advice that can truly make a difference in people's lives. It is not an easy path to take for the reader because it means the reader also has to be honest to themselves.

How can you argue with the idea that small constant steps will eventually take you to your goal, and not taking any steps won't? It is such a simple concept – but it takes a whole book to make some people truly understand it.

People who read "The Slight Edge" can achieve a positive difference in their lives – but not without some work from their own side.

Conclusion

"The Slight Edge" is a very helpful book if you can live with the fact that the basic points are stretched out over a variety of chapters. The book might benefit from adding some more exercises at the end of each chapter – because if you spell out everything in such detail, then it would also make sense to add exercises so that people can understand the ideas even better.

For people who are absolutely new to the personal development literature market, this would be the best book to start with, and for people who have tried many "secrets" before, this might be the last book they need to make all the others work. However, this book is also not a miracle course. It is honest right from the start (which many books are not): it tells the reader that it is up to him or her to make a difference, and that it will require work. The honesty in "The Slight Edge" by Jeff Olson is something that positively sets it apart from other books in the genre.

Thanks for Reading

Hello, this message is from the readers and writers at Summary Station. We hope that you enjoyed this summary/analysis and that it has helped your life in some way. It is our intention to create information that our readers will find useful and valuable.

We fell grateful for the opportunity to have people read our books and we are even more grateful when our customers leave a review. Please leave a review that lets us know what you liked about this book so that we can work on improving future books. Thanks again for your time.

About Summary Station

Many great books are released every year and most avid readers know that they never have time to read all of the books on their list. In today's world many people do not get as much time to read as they would like, so it is important to use any reading time wisely. The problem with this is that it can be very difficult to know if a book is worth reading until you have already invested some time into reading it.

This is one of the many reasons that Summary Station was created. The staff at Summary Station wants to provide readers with a way to get a good idea of a book before they invest their time and money into reading it. We make sure to provide you with as much information about a book as we possibly can, without giving away the ending or any other crucial spoilers.

With Summary Station you can be assured that you will not only get a quality summary of a featured book, but you will also receive valuable information and analysis. The themes and characters are discussed in each summary as well as a brief review of the featured book. Even if you know you are going to definitely read a book, it will give you a big advantage in understanding the book if you explore one of our excellent summaries first.

Preview of a Summary of "The Happiness Advantage" by Shawn Achor

The name of Shawn Achor's first book is "The Happiness Advantage: The Seven Principles of Positive Psychology that Fuel Success and Performance at Work" and it was released in September of 2010. This book was published by Random House LLC and it has remained on the bestseller list for quite some time. This book is responsible for changing the way that people from all over the world conduct their lives and careers.

This book starts out with Shawn explaining his experience at Harvard University. He explained how his gratitude for being able to attend one of the best universities in the world caused him to fall in love with the school. Looking back, he was able to determine that his experience at Harvard was significantly impacted by his enormous sense of gratitude for being selected to attend.

This insight was partly responsible for the inspiration behind the topics he would chose to research. Shawn points out the fact that Harvard is a very demanding university and most of the students who attend experience a great deal of stress due to these high expectations. A theory was formed and it basically stated that the students who do not have a sense of gratitude for being at Harvard become stressed easier.

This theory regarding gratitude has been formulated after

Shawn traveled the world to visit students from many environments that were very different from Harvard. He found that there were places in Africa where the students were genuinely grateful for their opportunity to attend school and they also enjoyed doing their school work. It was clear to Shawn that there was some kind of connection regarding gratitude and happiness, but it was still unclear as to what this information would determine.

Many people could not understand why Shawn decided to conduct his research on happiness at Harvard University because so many of the students there were already coming from a privileged life. Shawn realized that this was true, but he also realized that many of the same students who came from a privileged life were still getting depressed at Harvard. A search was conducted and the top performing students were selected to take part in Shawn's research.

The reason Shawn decided to pick the top students for his

research is because he wanted to see if there was some connection between happiness and success. It was already a well known fact that many of the students who performed poorly on their school work at Harvard were the same students who were affected by depression. However, most people were under the impression that the depression was a result of poor academic ability and Shawn was beginning to suspect that poor academic ability was actually a result of depression.

Click Here To Check Out The Rest Of The Book

Check Out More Books By Summary Station

"A Fine and Dangerous Season" by Keith Raffel – Summary

"America: Imagine A World Without Her" by Dinesh D'Souza - Summary

"Long Knives" by Charles Rosenberg – Summary

"The Bird Eater" by Ania Ahlborn – Summary

"Flash Boys: A Wall Street Revolt" by Michael Lewis - Summary

"The Doctors Diet" by Travis Storks – Summary

"I Can See Clearly Now" by Dr. Wayne Dyer - Summary

"Think Like A Freak: The Authors of Freakonomics Offer to Retrain Your Brain" by Steven D. Levitt and Stephen J. Dubner - Summary

"Wheat Belly: Lose the Wheat, Lose the Weight, and Find your Path Back to Health" by William Davis M.D. -

Summary

"The Confidence Code: The Science and Art of Self-Assurance – What Women Should Know" by Katty Kay and Claire Shipman - Summary

"Everything is Bullshit: The Greatest Scams on Earth Revealed" by Priceonomics - Summary

CPSIA information can be obtained
at www.ICGtesting.com
Printed in the USA
LVOW04s1112140616
492464LV00060B/1110/P

9 781500 636777

A Pig in the *Wind*

by Julia Devanthery

illustrated by Elizabeth Wolf

Harcourt

Orlando   Boston   Dallas   Chicago   San Diego

Pig put on his hat.
"I will hike up the hill
with my kite," he said.

Then the wind came.
"Whish," said the wind.
Off went Pig's hat. In went
Pig's hat. In went Pig!

Pig put on his skates.
He said, "I will fix this.
I will glide up the hill on
my skates."

Then the wind came.
"Whish," said the wind.
Down slid Pig on his
skates. In went Pig!

Pig sat on his bike.
He said, "I will win. I
will ride up the hill on
my bike."

Then the wind came.
"Whish," said the wind.
Back skidded Pig on his
bike. In went Pig!

Pig said, "I will think
for a while."
He sat inside.

After a bit, Pig smiled
and said, "I know how to
make it to the top of
the hill!"

"The wind will not win
this time," Pig cried.
"I will drive up the hill
in my car!"

The wind came.

"Whish," said the wind.

Up went Pig in his car.

Pig made it to the top of the
hill. He grinned.

"The wind is fine up here,"
said Pig. "It's fine for my kite."